So, you want to be a decorator?

An insight into the varied careers for a decorator

Pete Wilkinson
www.fastandflawless.co.uk

First published in the United Kingdom in 2020

Copyright © Pete Wilkinson

Pete Wilkinson has asserted his right to be identified as the author of this work in accordance with the Copyright, Designs and Patents Act 1988

All rights reserved. No part of this publication may be reproduced, stored in a retrieval system, or transmitted in any form or by any means, electronic, mechanical, photocopying, recording or otherwise, without prior permission of the copyright owner.

This book is not intended to provide personalised legal, financial, or investment advice. The Author and Publisher specifically disclaim any liability, loss or risk which is incurred as a consequence, directly or indirectly of the use and application of any contents of this work.

First Edition

18-09-2020

6X9

Contents

Preface

Chapter 1 — Introduction

What is this book all about?

Chapter 2 — How to get your dream job decorating

Whatever your age, here are the best routes into being a decorator.

Chapter 3 — Why "cards-in employment" is secure

The default choice once that you come out of your time, sick pay, holiday pay, regular hours, the "cards-in" route.

Chapter 4 — Self-employment — the blissful years

An insight into self-employment from the point of view of my 22-year-old self, back in the 1980s.

Contents

Chapter 5 — How to get the dream teaching job

How to get into teaching decorating if you feel that is a good career to take.

Chapter 6 — Why being in charge will make you stressed

Society expects you to do this but is it the best route for you?

Chapter 7 — Why you should create your own exclusive niche

An insight into self-employment the second time around. This time older and wiser.

Chapter 8 — Sprayer

Specialising as a sprayer, there are companies out there looking for you.

Chapter 9 — On-site training, NVQ assessor

This chapter looks at the word of the on-site assessor, how to get into it and what it is like out there being an assessor.

Chapter 10 — Author

An unlikely path, but one I have taken, so I share my experiences.

Contents

Chapter 11 — Estimator

If you are good with maths then this could be a great job for you, larger companies are looking for people to take on this role.

Chapter 12 — Building a decorating company

The ultimate choice for the experienced decorator, start your own company and build it big.

Chapter 13 — Social media and marketing consultant

Not really a typical job for a decorator but if you are good with social media you could carve out a career for yourself at a larger company.

Chapter 14 — Working on a large site as a subcontractor

This is a common route for the decorator, many companies employ subcontractor. Here is how the game is played.

Chapter 15 — Site Manager

Running a big site can pay well, here we look at the options for the decorator.

Chapter 16 — Working for a paint manufacturer

All your big paint manufacturers employ decorators, Crown, Dulux and Johnstone's will have a range of jobs that you may fancy.

Contents

Chapter 17 — Retirement

We have read a whole book about work and our career, here is a little bit about when you don't have to work anymore.

Chapter 18 — Some final thoughts

My take on a few things in our industry.

I dedicate this book to all the decorators out there trying to improve their business, their lives, and the lives of others.

Preface

When I was younger and working as a decorator at my firm, I didn't realise how many opportunities there were out there for me. I just thought that I would work at my decorating firm all my life working as a decorator.

This is not a bad thing and many guys that I served my time with are still at the same firm and happy decorating. It's good to know, however, what the options are and what other things you could do if you wanted to build your career.

In this book, I have tried to give you a wide range of possible options and I have outlined the best way to get into those careers. Some jobs I have done myself, so I have

Preface

a lot of experience of them and some jobs I have just come across along the way and I know people that do them.

I have also included some "off the wall" choices so that you realise that you could branch out and do something different but still use your decorating experience.

The two I have included are author and social media consultant. I have experience of being an author, so it made sense to write about it. I also have experience of decorators that are brilliant at social media and have made careers of it, so I thought I would include that in the book, too.

So welcome to the world of decorating, I hope that you find a path that you find rewarding for yourself.

Chapter 1

Introduction – What is this book all about?

Introduction

So, you want to be a decorator?

What kind of title is that for a book? What is the book about anyway? Well, I have been decorating all my life and I thought it would be good to give you an insight into the industry and what career paths you can take.

If you fancy being a decorator, then this book will give you some useful knowledge of what it involves and what you could do. I have done many decorating related jobs over the years, and I will talk about some of them here.

When I was seventeen and I was serving my time as a decorator, I bumped into an old school friend. He was studying at college and he was set to go to university to get a degree. He asked me what I was doing.

"I am training to be a decorator," I told him.

His reply has stuck with me to this day and at the time it really hurt. I didn't show it, of course.

"Dead-end job," was his reply.

Wow, dead-end. I had not considered my choice of work to be dead-end. I thought about this for quite a while after. What did he mean? He meant that once I had served my time as a decorator and was on full money then that was it. I would be a decorator all my life and be on the same money and there was no progression.

Is this true? I thought to myself.

Introduction

Remember I was only seventeen and a sensitive soul. Not very confident either. I decided that I liked the job I was doing, and I would stick at it. The thought of going to university did not appeal. This was in the eighties, too, when you didn't have to pay £9,000 per year to do one.

In those days, my younger self had no idea what possible career paths I could take. Looking back now nearly forty years later I have a lot more perspective. I have done several jobs over the years that are all decorating related and I know a few decorators that have done various types of work.

What I want to do with this book is explore some avenues that are open to you. I know different types of people will be reading this book. Different ages perhaps and with different backgrounds.

You may be a school-leaver and you have thought about doing a trade, you have seen this book and decided to check out what decorating has to offer you. If so, I hope that I can give you a real insight into the job and its rewards but also where you could be after a lifetime of decorating if you wanted.

I used to teach students that were still at school. These students were often in their final year at school. Many had decided on what they would do for a living. I remember one class in particular. A rather rowdy looking group of lads. I was covering the class for someone else, so I would only be taking them for one session.

Introduction

They looked at me as if to say, "what is this guy going to be like?" I chatted with the group first to see what they were planning on doing. I went around the class. It went something like this.

Joiner, electrician, electrician, plumber, bricklayer, electrician. You get the idea. No decorators. This would be a tough crowd. I decided to take a little risk and do some spraying with the group. This could go either way, they could just mess about and damage the equipment, or they could enjoy it and do some good work.

I showed them a video first and then talked about what they would be doing. I also talked about types of work that a decorator does and some typical earnings.

We went into the workshop and prepared some doors, then we set up the spray equipment and sprayed them. The lads were amazing, they did a fantastic job of their doors, they didn't mess about and they enjoyed the class.

Result.

When they had all gone, one lad hung back to speak to me. He had never considered being a decorator but, after the class he had just done, he had changed his mind and he thought it would be a cool thing to do.

I was so pleased that he had enjoyed the session so much that he had changed his career choice.

Introduction

You may be an apprentice decorator and you are studying at college on a day release basis. Maybe your teacher has given you this book to give you some ideas about where the job may lead. Many of the apprentices that I used to teach would ask me about what they could do when they had completed their apprenticeship. My advice was always the same.

Get some experience of the trade first. Whatever you decide to do in the future, if it is related to decorating then a good solid practical background will put you in good stead.

Sometimes apprentices would ask "What is the best job?" they meant what is the best job out there if you could do anything in any industry.

This is a good question and I had to think about it before giving a reply. I mean, what is the best job? Surgeon? Not if you don't like blood it isn't. Air traffic controller? Not if you can't work under extreme pressure. Premiership footballer? Not if you hate sport.

We discussed a range of jobs and what you begin to realise is that there is no one perfect job out there. You need to find a job that matches your personality. What do you like doing? What motivates you? These days it seems like everyone is only motivated by money therefore the job that earns the most money is the best.

People who have made a lot of money realise that this is nonsense. Steve Jobs said "The only way to do great work

Introduction

is to love what you do. If you haven't found it yet, keep looking. As with all matters of the heart you'll know when you find it."

Steve Jobs net worth when he died was $10.2 billion.

Choose something that you're good at, something that matches your personality and something that you enjoy. Okay, I know if you are painting every day then some days it can feel like a chore. Guess what? All jobs are like that. Hollywood actor? Some days you're sat waiting to do your bit. Tedious.

My son is a software engineer and he programs game software. Some days the job gets tedious, he has a mathematical mind and the job satisfies that to some extent but day-to-day it can get boring.

It has taken me a lifetime to realise what my personality is like and what job matches that. I am an introvert, so I don't like being in a situation where there are lots of people. Is this a good personality for a teacher, no it isn't? I struggle with every class I have ever done. I am out of my comfort zone and it leaves me exhausted. Would you ever know? Probably not, I am good at hiding it.

I am a big softie, so my feelings are easily hurt, and I don't like confrontation. I would be rubbish as a manager. I was a manager for a while, and I hated it and I was rubbish at it.

Introduction

These are all reasons that I packed in teaching and went back on the tools. It is probably the reason I like to write books. I am on my own at the computer dreaming up new things to write. I love it. I would do it for nothing and, in most cases, I am doing. I just hope I am helping people.

What I am saying is that if you are an apprentice then make sure that decorating is the job that you want to do and that you are good at it and you enjoy it. It can be difficult when you're young because you have little experience to go on.

Usually, if you like doing something then you are good at it. The money is important, of course it is. This is the reason we go to work. Don't make it the only reason that you are doing the job, though.

Trust me on this one.

You may have worked in another industry. Retail is a good example. I feel that people who have worked in retail have a lot of the qualities that you need to be a good decorator. You are organised and well presented. You have good people skills because you are used to dealing with customers.

Retail is having a hard time at the moment for various reasons. The internet is having a devastating effect on the high street and shops are closing down. I think this is a shame and I also think it will come back in time. Amazon has bought a chain of real shops for the next phase of their world domination so that tells you something.

Introduction

The pay is not that great at the lower levels in retail either so a change of career could be a great idea. If you are in this position, then you have a couple of options open to you. You can still get an apprenticeship and companies will take you on. Some companies prefer apprentices that are over twenty so don't think that no one will give you a chance.

The pay in the first year is poor so you would have to factor that in. Maybe save up so that you can make it through that first year. Once you are in the second year as an older apprentice you will go onto minimum wage.

Once you are out of your time, of course, you will be on full money. I will talk about the salaries of the different jobs that decorators do in each chapter.

Another route would be to continue your current job and go to night school to learn decorating and get a qualification. These days this route is expensive and an evening only course can cost thousands. Check out your local college though and see what they offer.

Another disadvantage is that the qualification that you gain will not have a work-based element to it so it will not be recognised. You would have to gain a further qualification once you got a job as a decorator.

What I would say, though, is that if you are not sure if decorating is for you then a night school class can be the way to go. I know students that have done a course at college in the evening and then gone on to get a job for a company.

If you can get an apprenticeship, though, then this is the best route. Approach decorating companies and ask them if they have an opening for an apprentice. It would be worth contacting the CITB (Construction Industry Training Board) because they will have a list of employers in your area who usually take on apprentices.

Check out their website.

Finally, you may be an older worker who is semi-retired. For example, ex-police or army. I have taught a few people who fall into this category and they make great decorators. They usually have a pension and are set up in life, so money is no longer an issue.

They are intelligent and willing to learn. They also get enjoyment out of the work because, who wants to sit at home watching TV all day?

For this type of person, the best approach is to set up a business and specialise in something. Do a private course in your specialism and then get good at it.

You can always expand your skillset as time progresses and you get a feel for what your customers want. If this is you and you want some guidance then email me on pete@fastandflawless.co.uk and I will do what I can to point you in the right direction.

Introduction

Before we get on with the main event and look at all the career paths that you can take as a decorator, I want to say one last thing.

On the subject of how much you can earn, it turns out that over the period of my working life, I have earned £1.2 million. I am not sure where it all is now, though. I have calculated that using the following numbers.

£30,000 per annum X 40 years = £1.2 Million

Now, I know I was not earning £30,000 per year when I was an apprentice, but for a lot of my time at college and to this day I earn more than that, so I think it's a fair average salary for my career.

With that in mind let's take a journey through decorating land.

Chapter 2

How to get your dream job decorating

There are many ways that people get into decorating and for each person, there is a different story. My story began as a spotty teenager who left school and did not know what to do. I went to college to study "A" levels because that was the default thing to do.

I hated it.

I was rubbish at A-levels, they were too hard. I started skipping classes and before getting kicked out I left.

I was quite artistic at school and someone told me that you could train to be a signwriter. These guys could hand paint signs and it seemed like a cool job. My dad was a joiner and he was well-connected. He knew of a firm looking for a signwriter. He arranged an interview at the firm, and I got the job.

The company was Dennis Kehoe Limited, and they were a decorating firm. They employed around 30 to 40 decorators. They also had a couple of sprayers, some paper hangers and a signwriter. The signwriter was called "Wally" (no I have not made that up) and he was a character, to say the least.

I attended college one day a week to learn about decorating and I worked on a range of jobs. I was not always working with Wally. I did little signwriting in the early days.

We used to paint a lot of churches and as part of that job, we would repaint the statues. I used to work with Wally doing these. They would be brought back to the yard and we would work on them.

Wally had all the colours mixed up, flesh colour for the face and hands and various colours for the cloaks and stuff. We were in the middle of a big job, there were about thirty statues to do.

A typical hand-painted statue

The next thing, Wally went off sick. I was expected to carry on and finish the job. In at the deep end or what!

I managed and I think I did a good job. I must have done because I got more to do. I would have a few statues on the go at any one time and I would do all the hands and faces, then the cloaks and the like. I was using oil-based eggshell, so I had to leave it overnight to dry before I could cut in the next colour.

I was only an apprentice and I think I was earning about £40 a week. I later found out that my boss charged £200 a statue. This was in 1983 as well so it was a lot of money. I used to complete about five statues a week depending on the size of them.

Oh, if I only knew then what I know now.

One of the foremen on the church jobs did not like me. He was called Pete, too. I think it pissed him off that this 17-year-old had the cushy statue painting job while he was up and down a 100-foot scaffold all day emulsioning ceilings. One day, he said to me that some organ pipes painted by another apprentice (his favourite one) needed touching up.

He also told me "not to take all day!"

These organ pipes were a right mess. Another apprentice had made a right mess of them. They needed doing again really. I did the best I could to touch them up but was fearful about spending too long on them.

Later that day the boss came on the job and looked at these organ pipes. "Who has done these," he said, "they are a right mess."

"Oh, it was Pete Wilkinson," was the reply.

Reputation trashed, dirty looks all round and, let's face it, if I had tried to explain myself it would have made things worse. As you can see, I was scarred for life.

I worked for this company for five years and I got a lot of experience there. It put me in good stead for the future ahead of me. I didn't realise it at the time, but it was a great place to serve my time.

This was my entry into the world of decorating and looking back I was lucky. Back then there were a number of what I call proper decorating companies. By this, I mean that they did the full range of decorating work from domestic decorating through to commercial work such as shops, schools and hospitals.

Also, these companies trained new apprentices every year and the apprentice got to experience the full range of work. Serving your time at a proper company gave you the full range of skills and, if the company were serious about training you, they would make sure that you got to work on a wide range of work and with a wide range of skilled decorators.

These days the industry is different. There are basically three types of company out there.

One-man bands. These will sometimes take on an apprentice but if they do then they will only be able to give that trainee a limited range of work.

Small companies. These are rare, but they are out there. They employ four or five decorators and will take on an apprentice. The trainee will experience a wider range of work, depending on what kind of work the company does, and they will at least get to learn from five different people.

Large companies. Very large decorating companies do take on apprentices however the apprentice is likely to get a limited experience. These companies pull in the big bucks by doing volume work.

For example, painting the outside of houses on a full housing estate. These jobs can take a long time to complete and I have known apprentices who have painted fences for three years. Not helpful.

Proper decorating firms do exist, but they are the exception rather than the norm. Typically, an apprentice class of sixteen would have three working for their dad, four working for small companies and the rest working for big firms.

If you are looking to get into decorating, then the best route is by far the apprenticeship route unless, as previously discussed, you are later in your working life and semi-retired. To get an apprenticeship you need to find a company. If you register with the CITB on their website, then they can find you a company to train at.

This sounds great! Saves you doing any legwork. I would advise against this though and for two very good reasons.

First, in my experience, different people will fit in better at different companies. The best companies at employing apprentices knew the type of person that would match their company culture. It's hard to give a concrete example of this but I think you would know if you would fit into a company.

If you research which decorating companies in your area take apprentices and then look at their website. What kind of work do they do, what do they seem like as a company? Are they small and friendly and do interesting work or are they big and corporate and just do massive jobs?

I know apprentices that would hate it at a small friendly company, and they just want to go to work and work on a massive job and do the same every day. Others like a more varied workload. What type are you?

Once you get a feel from the website, approach the company. It is likely that they will interview you. You will get a feel for what they are like during this process.

Finally, if you get an offer from the company then have a chat with the other decorators that work there as this will give you the final insight into what the company is like.

I know that this seems like a lot of work, but I had so many apprentices that never settled at the firm where they were serving their time and it makes for an unhappy apprenticeship. The ones that liked were they were working did well and enjoyed their time training and went on to do great things.

You are better with no firm than a bad firm, again trust me on this. All it will do is put you off decorating for life.

Second, the companies that the CITB have on their books that have still not found an apprentice are most likely to be the very firms that everyone is avoiding like the plague. The CITB has a duty to fill all the apprentice posts that they have and although they are very good at making sure that the apprentice gets a good placement, at the end of the day all places need to be filled.

Be wary of this. If you are offered a place, then do some research yourself before accepting. It is worth going into your local college and speaking to the painting and decorating teacher. They will know all the companies and can give you some unbiased (hopefully) advice. You do not have to accept the first company that the CITB offer you.

Be aware that the problem that I had at the college where I worked was that there were more firms than young people that wanted apprenticeships. I could always place anyone who wanted a job, no problem.

Currently, it's a buyers' market for people who want to be an apprentice. If you are a competent person and you want to learn then you are doing the company as big a favour as they are giving you a chance. It's a two-way thing.

Some students who leave school do not want an apprenticeship, and they do a full-time course instead. I think they want an easier life and have 2 years at college before they enter the world of work. This is a mistake. If you get a place at a company when you are 16 you will be paid to go to college, and you will also have a job at the end of it.

Sometimes I find a full-time course for two years can do more harm than good and once the student completes the course, they can be less employable. I know that sounds wrong but it's true for lots of reasons that I will not go into here. Just be aware that this route is not always the best. If you are reading this as a parent who wants the best for their son or daughter then take heed, apprenticeship is best.

Chapter 3

Why cards-in employment is secure

Why cards-in employment is secure

Once that you are time served and you are a fully qualified decorator then you have several paths ahead of you. This, of course, is what this book is all about, and I will explore each one with the advantages and disadvantages of each.

We will start with the simplest of options which is a "cards-in" decorator. This means that you are on the books of the company and you are employed. You will have a contract and you will be expected to work so many hours a day, you will have set hours and you will be expected to work so many days a week. For this, you will get a wage.

You will also get paid holidays, usually 4 weeks plus bank holidays. You will get sick pay if you are off work with an illness. All these things are good, of course.

Typically, you will work 8-hour days usually from 8:00 am to 5:00 pm with a break for lunch. It varies from company to company. My old firm we did 7:30 am until 4:30 pm with half an hour for lunch. This was an 8.5-hour day, but we did a shorter day on Friday.

Pay varies widely too but typically you will earn around £11.60 an hour. This is £464 a week or £24,128 per annum.

The decorating company that I was with had all their decorators cards-in. However, this is less usual these days, and a lot of small decorating firms will have a core of employed workers and then many more subcontractors who are used when the company is busy. This minimises the risk to the company, but I feel is not the best strategy if you are trying to build a solid firm with a good reputation.

I feel that if you are going down the cards-in road, that means that you are looking for security and a steady income. In that case, you would be better looking for larger organisations that are looking to employ a decorator.

You would be surprised how many of these there are. Local councils will employ decorators, not as many as they used to because a lot of the work is now contracted out however they still have a core team for maintenance work.

We had a maintenance decorator at the college where I worked. He was a very good decorator who had worked for many years at a local decorating company. His job was to steadily repaint all the college. Classrooms and corridors. He set his own work schedule and did a very good job. The work was not very varied, but the pace was steady, and he was never really under any pressure to finish a job.

Any larger areas that needed doing quickly were done by contractors. This job would suit someone who liked a routine and did not want to be pressured to rush and get a job done to a deadline. The disadvantage, of course, is that you will never break any income records. Having said that, the pay and benefits were good compared to a decorating company.

Why cards-in employment is secure

Hospitals, too, have their own maintenance painters as do schools. One of my apprentices worked for a large private school. The school was in an old historic building and they employed four decorators. The work was interesting, and the facilities were good, they had a canteen and decent welfare areas.

I have just done a quick search to see what jobs are out there for someone looking for a job employed as a decorator. Quite a few came up and here is just one example.

Painter Decorator Featured
In partnership with totaljobs

- Fulflood, SO22 5DF
- £24K to £27K per annum (Dependent upon experience and suitability)
- Permanent
- Recently

Painter Decorator Location : You will be permanently working from HMP Winchester, Hampshire, SO22 5DF Salary : £24K to £27K per annum (Dependent upon experience and suitability) Contract Full time, Permanent We are Gov Facility Service Ltd, a non-profit company owned entirely by the...

Painter Decorator

£24K to £27K per annum (dependent upon experience and suitability)
Permanent
Recently

Painter Decorator: You will be permanently working from HMP Winchester, Hampshire, SO22 5DF Salary: £24K to £27K per annum (Dependent upon experience and suitability) Contract Full time, Permanent. We are GOV Facility Service Ltd, a non-profit company owned entirely by the...

Why cards-in employment is secure

This was May 2020, so the job will be gone now. If you are reading this book in 2025 then the pay will look dated. This was typical of the search results that came up. The salary range is consistent with what you would expect for that kind of job.

Chapter 4

Self-employment — the blissful years

Self-employment — the blissful years

I have been self-employed as a decorator twice in my life. Once when I was twenty-two and then when I was fifty.

Both times were different due to the two important factors of my age and experience. The reasons I went self-employed both times were the same though.

I wanted more control over my life.

I had been working at the decorating company where I served my time, and all was well. However, I felt I had gone as far as I could go. The contracts manager was the son of the boss so that job was not going to come up any time soon and, if I am honest, I did not fancy being a manager.

So, I went self-employed. It was surprisingly easy. I told everyone I knew that I was going to go on my own and picked up a couple of small jobs. I handed my notice on Friday and I was working for myself Monday.

I had a friend who was a bookkeeper and she gave me advice on what records to keep. I also informed the Inland Revenue, of course.

I was only young when I did this although of course at that age you think you can rule the world. I suppose that is an advantage in business. I was lucky that my wife at the time was a midwife, so she had a good job with a steady salary. This took the pressure off a little and it was not all down to me to pay the mortgage.

I did mainly small domestic work, decorating lounges and hallway landing and stairs. Some outsides, I didn't mind doing them back then. I took on a couple of small church jobs and did some signwriting and gilding.

The church was something that I had done a lot of when I was an apprentice, so I knew how to go about the work. There was scaffolding involved and quite a bit of stencilling and gilding. I only have old photos of the work; these were before the days of digital cameras and mobile phones.

I have included photos of the work on the next page.

Above — All the gilding work on this church was redone.

Self-employment — the blissful years

Above — halfway through doing this stencil design.

Self-employment — the blissful years

Above — decorative work in a church.

I carried out quite a bit of signwriting work and I have a passion for boats too so that led me to do some signwriting on boats. This is still common to this day as a lot of boaters like a more traditional approach. I do not do this type of work these days, I am just too rusty with my signwriting skills, however, I still get asked. Below is one example.

Self-employment — the blissful years

I worked hard, I worked all week, long days and some weekends if I needed to. I was hopeless at pricing, looking back I was far too cheap. I didn't really do any marketing. There was no social media back then either.

Word of mouth worked well for me though, I had a good reputation as a decorator because I had won a high-profile competition called SkillBuild (Google it, it is still going) and this had been splashed all over the local newspapers.

Above — working on the SkillBuild competition piece.

I never took any deposits and I always got paid, so I was lucky, I guess. I never took on any really big jobs, though, so I think that helped. The experience was a good one for me, which is why I did it again later in life.

Self-employment — the blissful years

I always felt I could have done it better.

On reflection, the best time to go self-employed is when you are young. There are several reasons for this. You usually will have fewer financial commitments, especially these days when young people seem to leave it later and later before settling down.

You have a lot of energy too, which you will need. Decorating is a physical job so being young is a big advantage. Climbing ladders and scaffolding keeps you fit.

You are more optimistic and idealistic too when you are younger which means you are not as fazed by self-employment and you have no problem seeing yourself building a bigger company and making a fortune.

This can be done, of course, if you want that. I know of a local decorator who set up his own company. The workload built up until the company was bought out by a larger company, which made the founder a millionaire. This is more common than you imagine, and I feel it is one reason why self-employment is worth exploring.

I was busy with work and I got a phone call from my old teacher at college who was now head of department for construction.

"There is a job going teaching painting and decorating and I think it would be perfect for you," he said.

Self-employment — the blissful years

Teaching was something I always fancied. It struck me as an easy job, it was well paid, and the holidays were really good. So, I applied and had an interview.

It was a temporary one-year contract and I got the job. I just looked at it as a big job that lasted a year. "I will just go back on the tools after a year," I thought to myself.

I was about to enter a different world. It is a good job that I was young and naïve otherwise I might have been a little scared.

Chapter 5

How to get the dream teaching job

I went into college before the start of the new term in September just to get the lay of the land and help out with enrolment. This is when it hit home that I had a lot to learn.

I would be teaching on a new course. This was called "Signwork" and would be a signwriting course for adult students. I had done the Signwork course myself a few years earlier at another college, so I knew what was on the course.

Teaching it was another thing, though. I expressed my concerns to my boss. "Don't worry, Pete, I will put something together for you to start you off."

The first Monday of the course soon came around. I was bright and early but then so were some of the students. They were all sat in a classroom waiting for me, there were some stragglers, so I was waiting for them.

"Sorry, Pete, I didn't get the chance to put anything together, I am sure you will be fine," my boss informed me ten minutes before the start of class.

In at the deep end then!

There was a big sheet of plywood that had been painted blue. It had the alphabet painted it on it too with a number system for drawing the letters. I was familiar with this system, so I thought it would make a good first lesson. I got some drawing boards, pencils and lining paper and entered the class.

Just so you know, I am a shy person. Introvert they call it these days. I am not comfortable in front of a crowd. Now, if you have met me you would not think this, but I can tell you it's true.

I stood in front of about twenty adults in a classroom. They were all looking eagerly at me. Then it hit me that I should be scared.

Too late for that.

"Good morning, everyone. My name is Pete and I will be teaching you signwriting this year."

So far so good.

They all got themselves set up with paper and a drawing board and I explained how to draw each letter. They soon got the hang of it and away they went.

Phew.

It is an interesting thing that by the end of the year I had got to know all the students well. I asked one of them on the last day how I came across that first morning. Did I seem nervous and unprepared?

"Well, to be honest, Pete, I was terrified myself. It was the first day of a course, I had not done anything like that since school and I didn't know anyone," she explained.

I had never considered that the students might be more nervous than me.

"How did I come across, though?" I asked.

"I thought you had been teaching all your life," she said.

Well, it just goes to show, sometimes you can overthink things. A big lesson for me that day.

Things settled down, I planned the course properly so that I knew that all the things that had to be covered on the syllabus would be covered.

It takes quite a bit of planning to organise a yearlong course. You need to write an overview of the year. This is called a "Scheme of work" and you have to plan each lesson. These are called "Lesson plans".

I was not qualified to teach, so I had to attend a night class alongside the job to do a teaching qualification. I found this extremely useful and it taught me all the nuts and bolts of teaching.

Back then (1992) teachers were on a contract called the "Silver book", I was on this contract too but it was only a temporary one-year contract. The conditions that lecturers had back then were rather good and it was one reason that they could attract the best out of the trades.

It took me a while to get my head around after being self-employed.

We had 6 weeks holiday in the summer, 3 weeks holiday at Christmas and 2 weeks at Easter. We also had a week off for every half-term. There were three half-terms a year.

The working week was 30 hours. Out of that 30 hours you were expected to teach for 21 hours. The rest of the time was for planning and marking.

The government at the time had decided that this was far too cushy, and things would change. They introduced new contracts that everyone had to sign.

Each college developed its own contract. This meant that some colleges had a contract remarkably similar to the old one. Our college, however, made big changes to the old contract and the new one was more like a normal job.

The long holidays went (yes, I know, no one ever believed me) the working week got longer, and the teaching workload got bigger. Many left the job around that time to either retire or go to a college with a better contract.

I am writing a book about my time at college, warts and all so maybe check it out once it's published.

I didn't just teach signwriting. Over the years I have taught Interior design, decorative techniques and decorating.

I have taught on the Building HNC (computing) and I have taught on the National Diploma courses.

Apprentices have formed the biggest part of my teaching workload and in recent years that is all I taught. I like teaching apprentices. They work for a decorating company for 4 days in the week and they come to college for 1 day.

This is called a day release course and I think it is the best way to learn decorating.

On the whole, my time at college was enjoyable and I learnt many things over the years and got to teach some great decorators, many of whom I am still in touch with today.

They have their own firms now, though.

How to get into teaching a trade

Chatting with people over the years it's obvious that everyone thinks that teaching painting and decorating at college is a doddle of a job. The students used to tell me, and my mates used to tell me as well so it must be true.

Quite a few decorators have asked me how they could get into teaching so that they too could enjoy all summer on holiday, a pension, and a nice monthly salary. Warm and dry in winter too.

In fairness, even though the job is not as good as it once was, it is still a good job. From my observations in the staff room while I was still there, no young people were coming into the job. I don't know if this is because young decorators are not aware of the job or that they think that the job is just too difficult so that they could not do it or that they think that you need a degree.

Before I start though you need to know that it is not a job for everyone. Many came and went frustrated by the bureaucracy and the unruly students. If you have just come off the tools to go into teaching, there is a raft of new skills that you need to acquire quickly.

These include using a computer, filling in forms and attending meetings, and planning and tracking all your classes.

A full-time member of staff will teach for 24 hours a week and prepare and mark for the rest of the time. You could be looking after several classes in that time, too. Typically, I was looking after about fifty students.

The best thing to do if you feel like you would like teaching is to sign up to an evening only teaching course and do some teaching practice at the same college. If you are lucky, they may even pay you to do the teaching practice that is part of the course.

The good thing about this approach is that you discover if teaching is for you and you also get a chance to impress the team so they may offer you more hours.

If you don't like it then you have gained some experience and a qualification, and you may change your mind when you are older.

Chapter 6

Why being in charge will make you stressed

When I was an apprentice in my late teens, I thought that there was a ladder that you had to climb.

No, not a real ladder, a career ladder.

You started as an apprentice, then you came out of your time and you were a tradesman. Then you wanted to be site foreman and then maybe contracts manager and then finally the boss.

That's right, isn't it? Each job, of course, is "better" than the last. A tradesman is better than an apprentice. A contracts manager is better than a foreman. You get the picture.

Why is each level better?

The conventional wisdom says that each level is better because each level pays more money and carries more responsibility. It also has more power.

The tradesman tells the apprentice what to do. The foreman tells the tradesman what to do and so on.

Finally, the higher the level the more interesting your job is supposed to be.

This is what we are told.

Well, I have climbed the ladder. Some of it on-site and some of it at college. Having worked in both areas I can tell you that each new higher level feels the same regardless of being on-site or at college. No, maybe at college it is worse.

My experience is that with each step up the ladder your life gets worse, not better. Although I would like to say at this point this may just be me. I am not suited to being in charge. It has taken me 50 years to realise that.

My personality does not fit with what you need to be like when you are in charge. I am a bit soft and I like people to be happy. I don't like confrontation, pressure or meetings. I am honest and I like to say it as I see it.

My experience of being in charge is that you have to coerce (bully) people into doing what needs to be done for you to fulfil what you have been asked to do as a manager. For example, if I am a contracts manager and, in a meeting, I agree to complete a job to an unrealistic deadline then I have to persuade the decorators to get a move on and get done by the deadline.

If they say, "it's not possible!" I cannot be honest and say, "I know, the boss is an unrealistic egomaniac", I have to say, "I am sure that if you like working here you will get it done".

Another thing is that the money in many cases is not better. Decorators are usually on an hourly rate. If they do 40 hours, then that is what they are paid for.

Once you get promoted, you find yourself on a salary. This means you get the same money a month for whatever hours you work. If you take the promotion seriously and you want to progress, then you will work more than the standard 40 hours.

Some teachers I know at college did 80-hour weeks just to keep on top of the management workload. Let us do some maths, I will use college as an example because I know that the best.

Lecturer £30,000 per year 37-hour week.

52 weeks minus 7 weeks holiday = 45 weeks

30,000 divided by 45 = £666 per week

£666 divided by 37.5 = £17.70

This is just under **£18 per hour**.

Now let's say the lecturer gets promoted to the next level, curriculum manager. They are now earning £35,000 per year. Happy days, another £5,000 per year.

Let's look at the maths again.

Lecturer £35,000 per year 50-hour week. You would easily do this is you were a manager. Some managers I know worked all weekend to keep up.

52 weeks minus 7 weeks holiday = 45 weeks

35,000 divided by 45 = £777 per week

£777 divided by 50 = £15.54

This is just over **£15 per hour**.

Plus, don't forget the additional hassle. If you worked an 80-hour week then you are down to almost minimum wage.

I know all the arguments for promotion, we get them rammed down our throats by everyone and their dog. All I am saying is that it is not for everyone and if you are doing it for the money there are better ways to earn money that being a manager.

The world of software is a different animal and there is a reason for this. In software, if you are a talented programmer (basically a foot soldier in the world of computers) then you are a very valuable thing.

To keep you doing what you are best at the company will pay you what you are worth. In some cases that could be a six-figure salary. Your manager may be paid less than you. Imagine that!

The Peter principle

Ironically, there is a term for this, and it is named after me. When I was younger, I thought maybe someone had caught wind of the fact I was a rubbish manager. In fact, it is named after a Canadian author called Lawrence Peter who developed the unorthodox concept.

I googled the term, even though I knew what it meant and here is the result.

Being in charge

🔊 Peter Principle
/ˈpiː.tə/

noun

the principle that members of a hierarchy are promoted until they reach the level at which they are no longer competent.

Peter Principle

The principle that members of a hierarchy are promoted until they reach the level that they are no longer competent.

It means that if you are a good decorator then you will get promoted to site foreman. When you are site foreman you will do less decorating or even no decorating. This is a shame because you were good at it.

Why didn't they promote someone who was a rubbish decorator but good at organising people?

If you are a good foreman then you will get promoted to site manager. The process continues until you reach a level where you struggle. At this point, you will not get promoted any further. You end up in a job you're so bad at that the company does not want you to go any further.

So, what is the answer then? I think you need to discover what you are good at and pursue that. If you are an amazing manager then go for it. If you are not, then focus on what you are good at and do not let people bully you into getting a promotion.

Chapter 7

Self-employment — why I created my own exclusive niche

I must be mad, I tell myself. I have given up a "secure" job at the college to go back on the tools as a self-employed decorator.

Well, I didn't do it all in one big leap of faith. It was more like two little steps. I would like to explain myself so that you have a better understanding of why people change their careers.

I have worked at college for many years and I have taught thousands of apprentices. This part of the job was the most rewarding and it is the reason that I went into teaching in the first place (plus the holidays, of course).

Unfortunately, when you work for a big public-funded body, many things are out of your control. It is like trying to do a good decorating job with your feet tied together. You know that you can do it but it's difficult with your legs tied (yeah, I know it should be hands tied).

Colleges come under the "further education" banner. Funding wise, the government love schools and universities but have forgotten all about colleges. The irony is that most people with skilled jobs in the economy learnt these skills at college.

When there are skills shortages (and there are a lot) then these skills can be gained in college. It seems crazy to me that the government is restricting the very engine of economic growth.

I experienced a period of redundancies and budget cuts. I also experienced a period of nastiness from higher management. People were being bullied and having nervous breakdowns. Myself included. Not just at my college, I might add, this seemed to be the new approach.

For this reason, my very supportive line manager at the time allowed me to drop my management position and go part-time.

What I experienced when I went part-time were two things.

First, there was a lot of work out there for decorators and there was a skill shortage. I had a lot of work and the work paid well (better than college) so it was happy days. I love decorating and I love being on the tools. I know that this is odd to most people who want a shirt-and-tie job but that's me.

Second, college became enjoyable again. I was only part-time, so I did not get bogged down with meetings and the like. I just went into college, taught the apprentices and then came home.

Great.

During my half teaching and half decorating years, I gained a lot of experience in decorating again. It was a funny experience. I was time served; I had worked on the tools for 10 years before starting at college. In my years at college full-time, something happened to me that I did not realise was happening.

I was falling out of touch with the industry.

Had you asked me in my full-time years what I knew about decorating, I would have said "everything"; that's how I felt. But when I went back on the tools, the world of decorating had changed, and I felt like I had a lot to learn again.

This was good, I like learning and I like to experiment with new techniques. I had taught spraying at college for many years and I had always vowed that if I ever went back on the tools then I would spray everything.

I bought myself an airless sprayer and away I went. My sprayer was like an ATM, it was a cash machine, that just kept printing money. It's funny because decorators ask me if they should buy a sprayer. When I tell them "yes" they still deliberate?

It's like, "buy this for £1000 and it will print money for you". "Mmm well... I don't know, it's a lot of money, I am not sure I can afford it."

"It prints money, you will be able to afford it."

I genuinely want decorators to do better in their business. I am near retirement now. Before I retire, I want to pass on all that I have learnt over the years.

Self-employment — why I created my own niche

For these reasons, I started doing some local on-site training. I know a lot of local decorators and they contacted me and asked if I would do some training for them. I accepted and I did quite a bit of this.

I realised that there was a need for this in the industry. This led to me meeting Ian Crump on Spraying Makes Sense and we set up PaintTech Training Academy. I have told this story in my book "Fast and Flawless — a guide to airless spraying" so I will not repeat it here.

The academy took off, and we did training in specially built academies, we had excellent reviews and it was well-received. The decorators that did the course went on to incorporate spraying into their businesses and they made more money.

A seriously good result.

But I was still part-time at college (I am not sure how I fit it all in!) and one Monday when I was sat at my desk, I had a phone call from my head of department.

"Please could you come to my office," he said.

I made my way to his office, went in and closed the door.

"Please sit down," he said in a stern voice.

I wondered what was going on, I was sure that everything was going fine with the students and they were progressing well.

"The principal has found out that you have your own training academy and it is a problem. You need to stop doing the private training or you need to resign from college," he said.

Tough one, eh? I was earning twice as much from my private work than the college was paying me, and yet they wanted me to pack it all in.

What would you have done?

I served my notice and left the college. While I loved all my years at college, that was the best thing I have ever done.

I don't blame anyone at college, it was a contractual thing and my head of department was a great guy who had always been supportive. I had told him about the academy when I set it up and he didn't see it as a problem.

In hindsight, I think it was meant to be, I was making more of a difference to the industry on my own than I ever did at college.

Self-employment the second time around was much easier than the first. There are a few reasons for this. I had done it before, so I knew what to expect. I knew what mistakes I made last time and I was not going to make them again. I was more secure money-wise, so I was not under any pressure to price low to get the work. Especially when I was still part-time at college. The part-time salary was enough to pay my bills and the business income was just extra.

Self-employment — why I created my own niche

I was older too, of course, and I think this gave me a better perspective on life and what I wanted from the business.

I had built up many contacts over the years teaching apprentices and this meant that I more or less knew every decorating company in Preston. This gave me an almost endless supply of work.

Finally, because I had specialised in spraying and this was catching on it meant that I became the "go-to" guy for all things spraying.

What did I do different the second time around? Well, I did several things differently. Some of these things I could not have done in the late eighties because they did not exist. Here is what you should consider.

Create your own niche

This was probably one of the biggest differences from the first time that I went self-employed. I specialised. I was not a painter and decorator, I was an "airless spraying specialist". Sounds expensive, doesn't it?

This meant that I could charge more, it meant that people chose me and there was no competition because I am the only "airless spraying specialist" in the area. I go into this idea in more depth in my previous book on pricing.

Get visible on social media

This has been a roller coaster for me. I first went on Twitter to follow decorators who were also spraying. Twitter is great, it's just a feed of short sound bites and I found it a friendly place.

Then I went on Facebook which is a bit more interactive. The great thing about social media is that you can reach your target market pretty easily and you can build a customer base with very little money.

It takes time and some skill, but it is something you need to get good at if you are a decorating business in the 21st century.

You need a pricing system

When I was in my early 20s, I was hopeless at pricing. I just guessed most of the time. This time around I had a system and I knew that my prices were consistent. I started lower and built up my prices as I became established.

You should not accept every job

Another big change was that I didn't always say "yes" to a job offer. If it did not meet my criteria for what I was looking for I would not even price it. This sent a clear signal out to customers that I was a specialist.

I didn't expect to get every job either. If you are getting 100% of the jobs that you quote then you are too cheap, it's as simple as that. You can only do so much and the harder you are to get then the more people want you as a decorator. Some people really would not take "No" for an answer and would get upset that I would not work for them.

Help others as much as you can

This does seem like the wrong thing to do. I would help people who wanted to do what I was doing. I even had one decorator tell me that he would take all my work off me. This made me smile because there is enough work for us all if we support each other.

I have always found that if I help decorators get better at what they do then the rewards come back tenfold. This is not why I do it but it's a nice reward.

It does not always come back as money either, you often get much more valuable things back. Contacts and contracts come to mind. And friendships and support. It's not always about the money.

You need to build a relationship with the suppliers

Do not take your suppliers for granted. They do a thankless job and we need them. When the lockdown occurred, one of the biggest problems that decorators who wanted to work had was getting paint. It's then that you realise how important a supplier is.

Build a relationship with your supplier, help them all you can, recommend them to your friends if they are good and pay them on time.

Out of all the career paths that I have taken, self-employment has been the best. It allows me to do the work in a way that I see fit and it gives me the freedom to create a business that I want.

There are risks but working for a company these days and it carries a bigger risk, with a click of their fingers you can be gone when they don't need you. But if you have your own business and you have your customer base then you are much more secure.

Build it right and you might even have something of value that you can sell.

Chapter 8

How to get a job as a sprayer

Before I start, I would like to say that I do not see spraying as something different from decorating. I see it as part of decorating.

When decorators say things like: "Oh, I don't spray", to me, that's like saying: "Oh, I only brush, I don't use a roller."

Now I know it's not quite the same but it's only decorators in the UK that think this way. If you spoke to an Australian decorator, he would have a sprayer as one of the tools he uses on the job depending on what that job was.

I have written a full book on spraying called "Fast and Flawless" so I will not cover any old ground here. If you are interested in spraying and you feel that it is something that you want to add to what you do then read the book, you will find everything that you need to know.

I also strongly recommend doing a course, there are plenty out there, especially if you are going to use airless spraying because it can be dangerous. Some of the more specialist areas like uPVC spraying and kitchen spraying have specialist courses available.

These days a sprayer is something that decorating companies are looking to employ as a speciality, like a paperhanger. Joinery companies too. There are some specialist spraying companies out there who employ sprayers.

I was messaged on LinkedIn by a company down south looking for people who could spray, he had numerous openings. I did a little research and found quite a few jobs. I have listed them below. I have listed a London one and a Warrington one for comparison of incomes.

This is going to be a growing market for employment and if you don't fancy working for yourself but you have experience spraying then you could work for one of these specialist companies and hone your skills.

It would mean that all the equipment would be provided, and you would get an insight into the systems that companies use when spraying work. The two jobs I have selected is an on-site sprayer and a uPVC sprayer, these are two of the biggest areas at the moment in the industry.

On Site Paint Sprayer

Infusion Support
London

Apply on LinkedIn

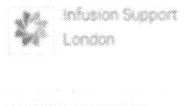

Over 1 month ago · Full-time

On Site Paint Sprayer

How to get a job as a sprayer

🕔 Over 1 month ago   📅 Full-time

On Site Paint Sprayer

On Site Paint Sprayer – Cladding, Roofs, Shop Fronts – Commercial Properties
Our client is seeking onsite specialist paint sprayers – re-spraying cladding, roofing, commercial buildings.

We are currently looking for Paint Sprayers to join our growing team.

Positions offered in London and surrounding areas.

Department: Industrial

Project Location(s): London

Responsibilities

Your main duties will include:

– Ensuring surfaces are thoroughly prepped and sprayed, to ensure the spray painting is perfect first time.

– Working closely with your team, the contractor and other trades onsite.

– Clearing up and making sure all sites are left clean and tidy.

– Following health and safety protocol at all times.

– Working to deadlines to achieve flawless results.

Applicants Must Have The Following

– Airless spraying of a variety of coatings (ideally 2yrs experience or more)

– HVLP spraying of a variety of coatings (especially 2-pack paints)

– CSCS, IPAF and PASMA

– Full driving licence

Typical Pay for this Type of Work

reed.co.uk	Totaljobs	PayScale
£32k–38k per year	**£25k–38k** per year	**£7.70–14.40** per hour
Paint Sprayer	Paint Sprayer	Spray Painter
Based on local employers	Based on local employers	Based on local employers

How to get a job as a sprayer

The pay rates above are for London and will vary from company to company and also based on your experience.

You can see what they are looking for in a candidate, a CSCS card and a full driving licence. Plus, experience of airless and HVLP. Just 2 years' experience of airless spraying, which is not a massive amount.

There will not be many with site experience of both HVLP and airless as these are two different markets.

The job below is for a uPVC sprayer. I think there will be a lot of jobs in this area in the future. It is interesting that they are looking for 2 years' experience, but this is preferred, so they will accept less if you can convince them that you can do the job.

This job is in Warrington and the pay is between £25,000 to £30,000 per year. I think that is good for a "cards-in" job.

UPVC Sprayer for domestic homes and Comercial properties

UPVC RENOVATIONS Ltd
Warrington

Apply on Amazejobs.co

23 days ago   Full-time

Ideally hold certificates and NVQ within this sector.

Job Type: Full-time

Salary: £25,000.00 to £30,000.00 /year

Experience:
- UPVC Spraying: 2 years (Preferred)

Flexible Working Options Available:
- Not offered

Work remotely:
- Yes

Report this listing

UPVC RENOVATIONS Ltd

More jobs at UPVC RENOVATIONS Ltd

See web results for UPVC RENOVATIONS Ltd

Chapter 9

How to become an on-site assessor

One career that you can follow if you are an experienced decorator is NVQ assessor or on-site assessor.

Before we talk about the role, I will give you a little background. Many years ago, the government decided that compared to other countries we did not have a very qualified workforce. This was not just in construction either it was in many areas.

To remedy this, it was decided to introduce a new type of qualification designed to be delivered in the workplace and it was called an NVQ or National Vocational Qualification. Experienced workers could be assessed in the workplace doing their job and then get a qualification.

If you were an apprentice in the workplace you too could be trained and then assessed and be given an NVQ. In many industries, hotels and hospitality, for example, the workplace model worked well, and training took place at the hotel by trainer/assessors.

In the construction industry, however, it was less well-received, and colleges took up the slack and delivered NVQ qualifications both for apprentices and in the workplace for experienced workers.

NVQs are often misunderstood and phrases like "NVQs are not like the old City and Guilds" are bandied about. City and Guilds are still the awarding body for NVQ and an NVQ is just a type of qualification like an A-level or a GCSE. In fairness, some of the early NVQ's were poorly written but on the whole, it is not a bad process.

Colleges took on assessors from each trade so that they could go out and assess experienced workers on site. The job has the best of both worlds in that you are like a teacher in that you have assessments to do and you go out and see students but all your students are older and wiser and you do not have to manage a class of unruly 16-year-olds.

You spend a lot of time out on the road, you will have a caseload of say sixty learners who you have to go out and assess. You will manage your own time and you will make appointments with students out on site. If you are good at it, you can have a bunch of appointments on one site or in a similar location so that you are not wasting too much time travelling.

The NVQ's are at different levels, the most common being level 2 and level 3. Most qualified decorators are qualified to level 2, some will have level 3.

The NVQ is made of several units: level 2 in Painting and Decorating has six units. Three units are "core" and these are done by all trades, such as the bricklayers and the joiners. These are things like health and safety. Some units are occupational and are specific to the trade. The units do change every so often and we are in the middle of a change now so I will likely have to update the book with the new changes.

If you are interested in this, then subscribe to my newsletter (details at the back of the book) and I will send out any updates.

Your job as an assessor is to gather evidence from the student so that you can prove that they can do the job. The units give you guidance so that you know what evidence to gather.

Forms of evidence include photographs, videos, documentation and witness testimony. Witness testimony would be your boss writing a letter to say that you had done some wallpapering, and he saw you do it and he was happy with it.

Evidence has to be mapped to the qualification and this can sometimes be tedious but there are ways to make it easier. There are software packages that help the process. We used to use a piece of software called "OneFile".

On OneFile, you could upload photos and videos and it linked the evidence to the right unit. The students could also log in to OneFile and answer questions and also upload photos.

This process can be the biggest part of the job. Once you have been on-site and got some video then you can come back to base and put all the evidence on OneFile. Base in many cases is home and many assessors work from home.

Here is an example of an assessor job.

How to become an on-site assessor

Construction - NVQ Assessor / Verifier – Levels 1-6
LV College
London NW1

£30,000 - £55,000 a year

- Easily apply to this job
  - Attending meetings with other assessors.
  - Development opportunities to deliver other training programmes and train other assessors.
  - A1/A2, V1/V2 or.

30+ days ago · Save job

This is London don't forget so a typical salary would be more like £30K. Some training providers will pay you on your workload. So, for example, so much per student that you complete.

This is an example of some things you will be expected to do, taken from the same ad on the next page. A lot of it is waffle but you can see that your main tasks will be observing candidates in the workplace, creating and assessing candidates' portfolios and keeping records of a candidate's progress.

The skills are self-explanatory, and you need to look through the list and ask yourself if that is you. If, for example, you are not very organised and you are not great at communicating then maybe the job is not for you.

How to become an on-site assessor

Responsibilities and Duties

Your day-to-day tasks will vary but will include

- Online Portfolio Management and recording update and assessment decisions
- On site assessments and visits
- Diary management
- Promotion of the NVQ programmes
- Planning and delivering vocational training programmes and workshops
- Observing and assessing candidates in their workplace
- Creating and examining candidates' portfolios of evidence
- Questioning candidates about how they would deal with non-standard situations
- Providing feedback and offering advice if the standards are not met
- Signing off the award when all the requirements have been met
- Keeping records of candidates' progress
- Attending meetings with other assessors
- Working closely with training staff and candidates' managers

Qualifications and Skills

Skills Required

- Being able to work with candidates from different backgrounds
- Having good communication skills
- Being supportive and patient
- Being able to work alone or with a team
- Having interpersonal abilities
- Being able to create accurate reports
- Having interest in helping people to develop
- Being tactful and patient
- Being able to clearly explain complex topics
- Being well organised
- Able to manage portfolios and documentation

You will need qualifications for this job but not as many as you would think, you need to be qualified in your subject area, ideally to a level above what you are assessing. In our case, you would need to be qualified as a decorator to level 3. You will also need an assessor qualification. These days this is the "A1" award.

The A1 award can be done online and typically centres charge between £300 - £400 for the course. Your local college will also offer the course. You will need GCSE English and Maths to get on the course too.

How to become an on-site assessor

Being an assessor is very different to being a decorator but there are many advantages, you are dressed up most of the time and you get to manage your own time. You still get to be involved in decorating and you will meet decorators on site.

The benefits are good, and you will get a good salary, sick pay and a pension. It is a job that you can develop in and if you continue to develop yourself there would be promotion opportunities for you.

Chapter 10

Why you need to know about being an author

I gave this chapter a lot of thought. Do I include it, or shall I leave it out? When I used to teach apprentices, I asked one particular class how many of them read a book.

No hands went up.

How many do you think will write a book? Yes, that is just what I thought.

However, the world is changing. These days if you are going to be successful then you will spend some time getting together information for your website, you will also put together some information for your social media output.

All this means writing good content. What is the best way to be good at writing good content? Read some good books. I am bound to say that, though, aren't I?

There is a book in everyone that needs to be written. Even if you think that you are a rubbish writer, your story will be of interest to people, your lessons in life will help other people.

Most people won't bother though, it is just an impossible feat to most. But it isn't really. If you write a book about your expertise, then it will be between 30,000 and 50,000 words. This sounds a lot but if you write 1000 words a night then you have a book in a month.

Even if you write 1000 words a week as I did with my first book then it will only take you 30 weeks, that's 6 months.

What if it does not sell? This does not matter. You have achieved something that most people have not done. You would be a decorator who has written a book. There are probably about ten of us. Welcome to the club.

Why do it, though? Why bother?

Well, there are three reasons.

First, it will give you credibility in your industry, especially if you have specialised in something that people are interested in. If your book has any value, then people will learn from it and respect you for sharing the information. You will also become the "go-to" person when people are looking for that specialism.

A book is like a business card that people pay for. They tend not to throw it away after they have read it, either. Sometimes they even pass it on for you! They will spend hours reading it, and they will understand what makes you tick and what you can offer them.

They will trust you, too, so that if you are a decorator then people will be more likely to engage your services if they have read your book. I do a lot of work for other decorators, so this helps me a lot.

I specialise in spraying and many decorators would rather get me in than do it themselves. Having a book out on airless spraying makes me the default choice in my area. It makes me the default choice globally, but I am not too keen on travelling. Manchester is a bit far for me these days. Joking aside I have travelled all over the country from Edinburgh to Devon and even to the States.

Second, you will help people and give them inspiration. This is one of the main reasons I started to write. I didn't realise it at the time but over the years I can see that it has encouraged lots of decorators to step out of their comfort zone and do something different. The pricing book especially has made a lot of decorators think about how they go about their business and made them change their priorities.

Finally, you could make some extra money. How much? Well, it depends on a lot of things. If you are thinking of writing a book to retire then this is not the right reason. However, some authors do make a good living.

I am in a Facebook group of an author in the UK who writes "teach yourself guitar" books. He earns about £60K. Okay, he has a load of books out there, and he has been at it a while and it is all he does, but you can see the potential.

So, if I have got your interest, here are a few tips to get you started based on my experience.

Pick a topic that you know loads about. Maybe you specialise in painting period houses. Write about that. Maybe you have built a business from scratch to ten decorators. Write about the journey and what you have learnt. You will know if you have picked the right topic because you will enjoy writing about it.

Write a simple plan. I usually write a list of chapters first and add a few notes to each chapter heading. This makes sure that your book follows a logical order and it helps guide you once you start going. This is one of the most important steps. I spend the first evening doing this. Don't spend too long on the plan though, no more than one evening.

Don't overthink it. It does not have to be a masterpiece. People will enjoy it more if it's a bit rough around the edges. Just write and don't stop. Don't read it back until you have done your 1000 words. I usually write for a day and then read it back a week later. Then I have forgotten what I have written, and I am reading it with fresh eyes.

You could get someone you trust to read it, a mate or your wife/girlfriend. They can give you some feedback and make any corrections needed.

Write a bit every day or every week. Set a time slot for the task. When I wrote my first book I did it on a Monday night when my wife went food shopping. I wrote about 1000 words and it took me about an hour. I did this every week and it is surprising how fast it comes together. If you enjoy it then maybe do a bit every night. That way you will get into it and the book will come together faster.

Writing the book is only half the job. I didn't realise this at first. Once you have finished you need to proofread it and tweak it so that it reads well. This is very time-consuming, and it is difficult to do yourself. I pay a professional to do this for me now and it is the best thing I have done.

The job is completed in a few days and I know that it's been done right. You're probably looking at about £200 - £300 for a decent proof-reader depending on the number of words in your book.

Everyone judges a book by its cover. Get one designed by a professional. This is essential. If you design your own, it will not look great. You may think it does but when put alongside other books with professional covers then yours will stand out as amateurish.

Have a look online and see who is out there. You will be looking to pay anywhere between £100 to £500 for a cover. Beware of a cheap designer, though. I had a £100 cover designed and I helped so much it was my design and it was rubbish. I wasted £100.

I now use a company called "More Visual Ltd" and they are brilliant to deal with and the covers look great. You can change the design and change the colours until you are happy.

Why you need to know about being an author

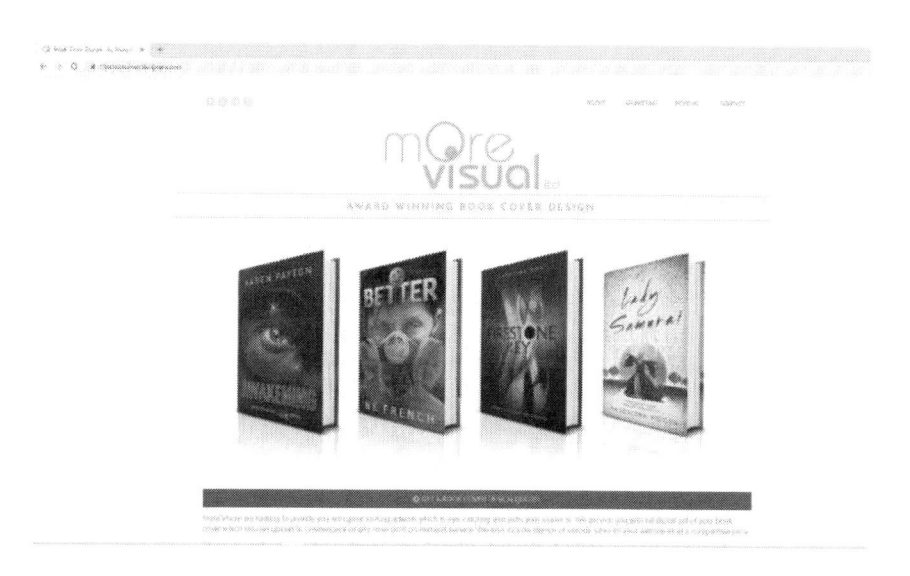

These days the cover is my favourite thing.

Once you have your book and it's been proofread, and you have a great cover then you can get it printed. The best way is to use Amazon. I won't go into it here because there is loads of guidance out there. You can use a printer and get your own copies printed. If you already use a printer for your business, then this could be a good option.

I did this in the early days, but it is slow and expensive. Once your books arrive (an exciting day, I can tell you) then it's time to give a load away. These are your pre-release readers who will give you feedback and spread the word for you too.

Marketing your book is a whole new ball game, and I won't go into it here, the main reason being that I am not an expert myself.

Finally, don't expect to get rich, then you won't be disappointed. Do it for the right reasons. If you have a hit and make some money, then that's a bonus.

If you're still with me and you're thinking about doing this but feel that you need some help, then I am prepared to ghostwrite the book for you. This means that you still have **your name** on the book, no one would know that I have helped.

I would do all the leg work, the copy-editing and proofreading and sort the cover and finally publish it for you.

There would be a few criteria that you would have to meet. These are:

- I would have to like the idea of the book.
- I would need to be convinced that you will complete the manuscript and that you are serious.
- I would want a negotiated share of the income generated after costs such as book cover design have been deducted.
- I would want a deposit upfront.

I am not looking for work, I am too busy really but if I can help you, then I will. Email me on pete@fastandflawless.co.uk if you're interested.

Chapter 11

Is an estimator an attractive career choice?

Is an estimator an attractive career choice?

Some decorating and building companies will employ an estimator. If this is something that you are good at then this could be the ideal job for you if you want to get off the tools.

I searched to see what jobs are currently out there (June 2020) and I found an "Assistant estimator" working for a contractor. The money was not bad, between £22K and £30K and you would get training and be able to progress to a higher salary.

The job also had a bonus scheme, so if your price is right and the job makes money then you would get a bonus and there was a pension also.

Here is the advert.

Assistant Estimator

Construction Jobs
Preston

Apply on Estimator Jobs   Apply on Construction Job...

⏱ 7 days ago 💼 Full-time

Preston, Lancashire

This North West based contractor, currently a number of high-profile projects underway in and around Lancashire,

Is an estimator an attractive career choice?

they are looking to strengthen their Estimating Department with the addition of an Assistant Estimator.

The contractor has an interesting and diverse workload including, social housing refurbishment, new build schools, refurbishment of law courts, hospital refurbishments, new build affordable housing and listed building refurbishments.

Our client realises that the way to attract the best estimators in the industry is to offer a combination of the best training, the best packages, and the best working environments.

Typical packages include:

Basic salary dependent on experience, but typically £22K - £30K

Car/allowance

Pension

Bonus for projects completed in time and on budget.

If you were serious about making this your career choice, then you would need to do several things. First, if you are a self-employed decorator then get good at pricing your jobs.

Here are ten pricing tips that you should follow:

Don't guess.

This is a trap that many decorators fall into, they guess how long the job will take and multiply that by a daily rate of pay. For example, the job will take 4 days at £120 a day so that's £480 plus paint. This is no good for small jobs it's certainly no good for a large job.

If you worked for a company as an estimator, they would expect you to work from a set of rates.

Learn how to measure up.

This is a useful skill. You need to be able to measure the area of the walls and ceiling plus the length of the skirting and architraves. You would then use this size to work out your price using your rates.

Many decorators that I have spoken to struggle with measuring up, so it's worth getting your head around it and getting good at it. It is easy once you have some practice.

Know your cost price.

This is something that decorators don't really understand. If you work out your time and materials and don't add anything on, then this is the amount it costs you to do the work. It should not be the actual price.

For example, if it costs DFS £300 to make a sofa, they don't sell it for £300. They sell it for whatever they can get, maybe £600.

You need to know your cost price because you need to know if you are making money or not.

Time everything that you do.

A professional estimator would use a price book or a book of rates to get industry standard times for various jobs. As a decorator, we can build up our own set of times so that we have an accurate idea of what our base time for doing a job is.

We can then match this time against the going rate for the job and see how profitable it is.

Get constant feedback from the market.

The price you can get for a decorating job is set by the market. This changes over time. For example, if there is a lot of decorating work about and everyone is busy then the price that you can charge for the work goes up.

If it's quiet and there is not much work around then the price that you can charge goes down.

It is difficult to know exactly what the market is doing because there are so many variables however you can keep your ear to the ground and keep an eye on what prices are doing. This means that your own estimating is informed.

Don't aim to get every job.

One way that you can get feedback is from your own prices. If you get every job, then you are too cheap. If you don't get any then you are too expensive. You want somewhere in-between.

Different companies will look for different percentages. For example, you may decide that you only want to get half of the jobs that you price for. So, that's 50%. Some may want 70% and some may be happy with 20%.

Get a deposit.

This is a controversial topic. I would say that you should get a deposit when booking a decorating job in. The percentage deposit is up to you. I would say that 50% is the upper limit, not many will give you more than that if you have not done any work. I usually charge 20% for the deposit and this covers my materials.

Have terms and conditions.

You need to have conditions attached to the price otherwise the customer will assume all sorts of things and usually to their benefit.

For example, if they cancel, do they get their deposit back? If they change their mind on the colour halfway through, then what happens then? If the woodwork needs a further coat because it has not covered is this in the price or is it extra?

You need something to refer to when things go wrong. If a customer signs your terms, then it is more difficult for them to say that they didn't understand what you were offering. Even if it is as simple as "I expect payment within 7 days".

Don't be too cheap.

Another trap that we all fall into. We feel like the customer is doing us a favour for giving us the work, so we want to be as cheap as possible. Don't do this. You will never get anywhere with your business and everyone will always see you as a cheap decorator and it will be a difficult label to lose.

Don't drop your price for no reason.

If you drop your price for no reason at all then you lose all credibility. They will think you were just trying it on. If they want it cheaper you could negotiate a lower specification, for example, cheaper paint or one coat of paint.

I would not even go down that road but at least you have a reason for the lower price. If you are always dropping your price to get work then something is wrong, you have your pricing system wrong or you are simply too soft. Don't do it.

Second, do a course in estimating or maybe get a higher qualification. There are a few out there, and they will teach you new concepts like SMM and NRM.

SMM is the Standard Method of Measurement and it has been developed by the Royal Institute of Chartered Surveyors to standardise how projects are costed. Quantity surveyors and estimators will use this so that everyone knows what standard is being followed. The rules are updated every 10 years the last being SMM7. This was not updated and was replaced by NRM.

NRM is the New Rules of Measurement and now supersedes SMM. You can see now why it would be good to do a course if you are going to get a job estimating or even get better at estimating in your own business.

To sum up, this is not for everyone. If you are good at pricing then you could look to gain employment in this area, if you have your own business then it is something that you need to master anyway.

Chapter 12

Is business perfect for you?

Is business perfect for you?

This is not a job, but it is a career option. One that I think will become more attractive as the job market changes in the next 20 years.

At what age would you start a business? The younger the better, I think. Although you have more experience when you're older, you have more reservations, too.

When I say build a company, I mean just that. I do not mean self-employed with a couple of subcontractor mates; we are building a proper decorating company with twenty-five employees or associates.

Over the last two years, I have been involved with a business development manager who served his time as a decorator. The company that he worked for went into liquidation, and he decided that rather than get another job, he would build a decorating business from the ground up.

He approached me because he wanted me to do some training with the team that he was going to build. I think that we both have learnt a lot along the journey, and we are still learning.

It is interesting because we share many views about the industry, and we differ on some aspects of running a business. I will discuss the journey and our differing views on certain aspects so that you can decide for yourself what you would like to do.

Before I tell the story, I want to discuss why you would build a company rather than work for someone in a job.

You never own your job. You can work for a company for many years and at the drop of a hat they can get rid of you or put you on the job from hell. They can pay you less, they can put someone in charge of you who is an idiot. Some people like that they can go to work and not worry about the business side of things. They feel that they are more secure in a job and that having a business would be risky.

I think the exact opposite. Working for someone is not secure, especially in today's world. I also do not think it is as risky to have your own business as it used to be. The start-up costs are less and there are so many ways to cheaply automate many of the office functions.

If you set up in business and you found that it was just not for you then you always have the option of going back to a job, although I don't think you would.

Let me get back to our decorating company example. The company was a new one and was set up in 2018. They took on a contracts manager, a training manager (me) and some decorators.

The work was three large contracts that were new-build apartments. There was a large volume of work and the jobs overlapped. We had a reasonable soft start, but the workload spooled up quickly.

The workforce was mainly subcontractors working on a price. As the work increased the number of decorators increased and over quite a short space of time there were fifty decorators. This is fast by anyone's standards. The wage bill a week was around £30,000.

Mind-blowing (well, for me, anyway).

From my point of view, the things that I would do differently are as follows.

First, I would employ the decorators and not subcontract them. I may have a core of, say, twenty-five employed with the buffer of subbies. I would pay them a good salary, around £35K. This is less than the price guys were earning but more than an average "card in" person.

I would set targets for production, let's say two apartments a week and give a bonus per week if the target was met with no snags.

The advantage of this is that no one would rush the work because they are on a price and you could have set times that they arrived and left so that it would be easier to manage the team.

Second, I would build up more slowly so that each new decorator that is added to the team is carefully vetted. It is easier said than done sometimes if you are offered a big job and you need to get up and running quickly. A team takes time to develop and a couple of misfit decorators can upset the balance of what you are trying to do.

Third, I would have a diverse portfolio of work so that I was not just working for one client. Ideally, you want several clients in each sector that you are working in. So, for example, four or five builders, maybe ten to twenty private clients. I also think that it is important to have a mix of work to keep things interesting for your team.

One thing that we do agree on is the use of systems to make sure that the large number of apartments that were being decorated were done to a consistent quality.

This was done in a couple of ways. First, a training programme was developed for each decorator to go through. This was delivered both off-site in a purpose-built training academy and also on-site to consolidate the learning and make sure that the decorator had understood what they had been taught and was carrying it out to a commercial standard.

Second, a booklet was written outlining the processes, procedure and products that we would be using and setting out the expectations for the decorators. This was a reference point that helped the decorators to revisit what they had been trained to do.

The main thing when building a decorating business is to have a plan of what you want to achieve and work to that plan. A plan will turn into your systems and your systems will give you the results that you want from your business.

Here are six tips to keep in mind when creating your systems and building your decorating company.

1. **Keep it simple**. No need to overcomplicate things, if a simple system does the job then that is the one that you want. It is easy to get carried away and make everything too complicated.

2. **Don't have a system for the sake of it.** Only have systems in place for what needs to be done. I would suggest the following as essential: Work systems, how best to carry out a job. Pricing systems, a clear set of rates and method for pricing. Marketing systems, how you bring in new customers. Recruitment systems, this is for taking on new decorators.

3. **Test your systems and revamp them when needed.** This is very important. You must measure your results and if the results slip then you need to look at the process again.

4. **Write the system down.** Ideally have an operation manual, one for the decorators and one for the office. That way everyone knows what they are doing without having to bother you.

5. **Don't become a slave to your system.** You are the boss. If something is not working or is counterproductive then get rid of it. Circumstances change, so your system may stop working. Be aware that this may happen.

6. **Make sure that your systems are right**. For example, if you are using a new paint system on a contract then check with the manufacturer that you have understood how it should be carried out before going ahead.

Is business perfect for you?

Much of this is explored in more detail in "Fast and Flawless Systems".

Chapter 13

Social media and marketing consultant

Social media and marketing consultant

This is a book about career paths for decorators and here we are with a chapter on being a social media consultant. Sounds complicated, doesn't it?

I will be honest, and say that I am not sure about this one. It's all very new at the moment and there are jobs out there, but I am not sure if you would get into a company without some social media qualification.

I searched on the internet to see what jobs there were out there and I found this:

Content Marketing / Social Media Manager

Posted 5 June by RSM Agency

£22,000 - £35,000 per annum Bolton, Lancashire
Permanent, full-time

Content Marketing / Social Media Manager

Want to work for a small, dynamic, integrated marketing agency; where we believe hard work, gets reward?

Our client has been trading for over 20 years' working for some of the world's largest brands; Mercedes-Benz, Sony, Ford Motor Co., Yamaha, Michelin, Lamborghini to name a few. As part of a close-knit team you will be involved in a fast-paced, creative environment, where quality is key.

They are looking for a Social Media Manager to join their small dynamic team based in Bolton; who enjoys a 'can do' approach, and a passion for both digital marketing and self-development.

Position: Content Marketing / Social Media Manage
Location: Bolton, BL3 5AB
Job type: Full Time, Permanent
Salary: £22,000 to £35,000 per annum dependent on experience

Social media and marketing consultant

The above job is a general social marketing manager and I don't think that would be suitable for our purposes, but I think this could happen in the future.

Large decorating companies have a social media output and in fairness some of it is good but some of it is not great. A decorator who has experience of how jobs are done and also has experience of products and how they perform would be good at producing interesting posts that would appeal to both customers and the trade.

A lot of social media is just that: social. How it works is that it is like going to a party where there are customers, potential customers and fellow workmates who work for you or maybe want to work for you. Plus a few random people that have lost their way and wonder why they are at a party full of construction people.

So, it's your job to do a few things at this party for your company. You must appear that you are a good company and you are professional. So, no swearing or getting drunk.

You have to try and get some new work from the potential customers in there. You have to maybe attract some high calibre decorators to come and work for your company.

How do you do this?

Well, what you wouldn't do is walk up to each person at the party and talk about yourself and your company and then ask if they want any decorating done. That would be a turn off for everyone.

You would try and relate to people and chat about them. Why they are at the party, what they have to offer. Then hopefully they will do the same for you. If you have mutual needs, then you may do some business.

If you are a decorator yourself it is far easier to speak the same language of other decorators and even customers. You have real-life experience of decorating work and you can relate some stories to your potential customers.

This is exactly the way social media works. You need to speak the language of the trade to be engaging and successful. For this reason, I think that you could get the job for a larger firm managing their social media.

Okay, you will need to learn the technical side of things. Things like writing blogs and running email campaigns. But it is only like when I started at college and I had to get my head around registers and schemes of work. You would get into it.

I will tell you something now that not many people know. I worked as a software engineer for a large software company writing software. Wow! How did I pull that off?

Well, it was not that difficult. When I was at college teaching sign making, I had to use a computer to do the computer-aided sign making part of the course.

I was 27 and I had never used a computer in my life, this was 1992 so it was not like it is today. I had some training

Social media and marketing consultant

from the supplier of the sign making software and I spent some time on the computer.

I found that not only did I enjoy it, but I was also good at it. I bought myself a computer for home and got more familiar with it. I then dabbled in some simple programming. Again, I was pretty good at it, so I did a course at college.

I did a 2-year HNC in computing. This covered all aspects of computing such as Word and Excel but in the second year, I specialised in software engineering which included software design and C++ programming.

Then one student on the course told me that his company was looking to take some people on and if he recruited me, then he would get a recruitment bonus (£1000) and he would split it with me.

I went for an interview and I got the job! I was programming in a language called COBOL. Most banking software is written in this, plus most of the government computer systems at the time. COBOL code manages financial transactions every day all over the world. There are twenty times more transactions processed by COBOL than there are Google searches a day!!

Anyway, I got the job and held it down for a few years. I got a big bonus after one project and got a promotion too, so I must not have too bad at it.

In the end, I went back to college, I found that I didn't like being too tied to a desk all day and I missed the decorating.

It was an adventure, though.

If you are good at something and you really fancy doing it then you can make it happen. You might have to hone your skills in your own time, and you might have to get a qualification too but it's possible.

Chapter 14

Would you like working on large building sites as a subcontractor?

Working on large building sites as a subcontractor

If you are a decorator, then it is likely that you are also a subcontractor. About half of all construction workers are either self-employed or subcontractors.

If you are working on a large site, then it is likely that you will be a subcontractor. Sites by their very nature are temporary things. Companies balance this risk by having a few cards-in decorators and many subcontractors.

Many people shy away from being a subcontractor and prefer to be employed. The reasons for this are that they see subcontracting on a large site as a hassle. They also see it as insecure.

In fairness this can be true, some builders can be difficult to work for because they are disorganised and like to bully the decorators. Decorators often must follow substandard trades and then put their work right for no extra money.

It can also be a culture shock if you are used to working on domestic decorating jobs where you can park your van on the front and have easy access to your tools.

Suddenly, you are on massive site; your van is parked miles away and you have to carry all your tools with you. You cannot leave anything anywhere or it will go walkabout.

What you will find though is that you get used to it. You settle into a routine; you get to know the site managers and other trades and before you know you are part of a team. If you were working for a decent building company then you could be part of a great team.

Large decorating companies struggle to get good decorators so if you are a half-decent decorator, they will snap you up.

If you are good at your job, they may even take you on full time if you want that. Many decorators like the flexibility that being a subcontractor gives them. They are usually on a price and this means they can come and go as they please as long as they meet agreed production targets.

Let me give you an example. Let's say that you are decorating apartments in a large tower block. There are hundreds to go at. You will be part of a team, though, so you will not be expected to do them all.

The price for the apartments will vary from company to company but just as an average let's say that you get £400 per apartment.

It is up to you how much you want to earn and how fast you are at painting them. The great thing is that you do not have to supply any materials or wait for your money. You will generally be paid a week in hand the same as a cards-in decorator.

If you are not that money motivated and you have a sensible number of outgoings you may do one apartment a week and be happy with your £400. You could easily do this in 3 days and have a 4-day weekend every week. How good is that!

Working on large building sites as a subcontractor

You may do three a fortnight, so one and a half a week. This way you earn £600 a week, which is actually above the national average. You would do this in just over 4 days per week so you could still have your nice long weekend.

You get the picture. As long as you don't agree to do three a week and then disappear off after one, your employer will be happy.

If you are good at doing the work and you produce a high-quality finish in a sensible time, then your employer will want you to work 7 days a week. If you want this, then that's up to you. There will be enough work for you, and you could earn some good money.

If, however you have a life and want a better balance then you should have this discussion before you start and then the employer knows you have asked for that. After a while, they will get used to your routine and leave you to it.

When I was working on-site, I agreed I would work 4 days, Monday through to Thursday. I had Friday off every week, this is something the other trades could not quite get their head around. In fairness, I could not get my head around why someone like a highly paid electrician would work 5 days but there you go.

To set up as a subcontractor there are several things that you must do, none of them complicated.

Working on large building sites as a subcontractor

You need to be self-employed and let the Inland Revenue know. They will issue you with a unique taxpayer reference or UTR. The decorating company will need this number to pay you.

Your company will deduct 20% tax from what they pay you. This is too much because you can earn £12,500 before you pay any tax. When you fill in your tax return and submit it you will get some tax back. Many subcontractors use this tax back as holiday money and go away for a couple of weeks in April or May with their tax rebate.

If you are worried about doing the tax return there is no need to because if you are a subcontractor then an accountant will only charge you about £100 to do your tax return for you, well worth letting them do it, I feel.

You will also need an NVQ level 2 in decorating to get on site. There are ways around this but if you are a time served decorator you should have it. If you have been decorating for many years but have never got qualified, then you get to be assessed on-site. Many training companies will do this for free.

If you are unsure of which company to use then email me on pete@fastandflawless.co.uk and I will point you in the right direction.

Once you have your NVQ level 2, you will need a CSCS card. CSCS stands for Construction Skills Certification Scheme. It is a card with your photo on which shows that you are qualified in your trade and that you have done some recent health and safety training.

The card has to be updated every 5 years. They are fairly cheap to get hold of. You pay for a health and safety test, this is about £30, and you pay for the card once you have passed the test, and these are about £20.

You will be asked for this card when you do the site induction and the building company will take the details from your card and put it on their database.

If you are a decorator who is currently self-employed doing your own work and you fancy some site work, then it is easy to get sorted. Look around to see where the work is going on. Approach the site office and ask on the gate who the painting contractor is.

Once you know this you can contact the painting contractor and ask them if they are looking for decorators. If it is near the start of the job, then they are likely to be looking for decorators. I would do some background checking on the company to see what they are like to work for before rushing head-first and working for them.

A note on day rates. Site work is split into two. Price work and day work. Usually two sets of decorators. The day rate is for snagging and odd bits of work that are difficult to price. The day rate that the decorating company will pay you can be negotiated. It will typically vary between £120 and £150 at the time of writing.

Before you get too greedy when negotiating the day rate remember that it will be paid every week, guaranteed. That is worth something. If you are brilliant and you start at a lower rate, then you could negotiate higher once the company realises what a superstar you are.

To earn the big bucks, you need to be on a price. Be careful here though because some firms can be a bit underhanded. If you smash it out of the park and do 4 apartments, they may be reluctant to pay you 2 grand a week.

What may happen is that they take you off price and put you on a day rate, or they may just cut everyone's rate. There is no point getting all worked up about it, this is just the way some firms operate. Ask around, find out what the other guys do. I would just work steady, do a good job and earn a reasonable wage without getting too greedy.

I did some research and at the time of writing (2020) here is where most of the work is:

Region	Percentage of UK building work
South East	15%
London	14%
North West	12%

As you can see, nearly half of all the building work going on is in just three regions. Surprisingly, London is not in the top spot. Also surprisingly, the North West is up there with the big boys.

Just for comparison, the North East only has 3% of the building work being carried out.

So, if you are struggling to find something in your area then maybe check out some of the hot spots.

You may have to do your own research if you are reading this book in 2025.

Chapter 15

Site Manager

Site Manager

If you are a qualified decorator and you have been working for a while at a company then you may be thinking what your next step should be. The most obvious is to move up to management. There are several ways that you can do this.

The simplest is to become a site foreman for the painting company that you work for. If you are thinking of going all the way and becoming a site manager eventually then you would be better if you worked for a company that did site work. That way you will work with the construction company site managers and it will be easier for you to get qualified.

Let us look at why you would want to become a site manager before we look at how you go about it. There are three reasons why it is a good move.

First, there is always a shortage of good site managers. You would never be out of work. Because the role is in demand you can look around and find a good company to work for.

Second, the money is good. Depending on how good you are you could earn between £50,000 - £100,000 per year. There could be healthy bonuses too if the contract hits its targets.

Third, there would be an opportunity for career advancement. You could climb the ladder at the company that you are working for, you could move over to a bigger company and it will give you progression.

Site Manager

I always used to tell the apprentices to consider this route because of the money and the progression. In fairness, most site managers are ex joiners. However, I know a few who are ex decorators so don't be put off by this.

What are the best routes to a site manager job? It depends on where you are in your career as a decorator. There are four routes.

Route 1 — An apprenticeship

If you are young and you are doing an apprenticeship with a decorating company then once you have qualified and you are 18 you could apply for another apprenticeship at a building company to train as a site manager.

There are several advantages to this, the company will pay for you to go to college and then university to get your qualifications. The company will give you valuable paid work experience as you train and, once you have qualified, you will be offered a job.

Route 2 — A university course

If you have been to college and are qualified as a decorator to level 3, then you can go back to college on a day release basis and study towards a Higher National Diploma or HNC. This will take 2 years at college.

The course fees are quite steep (thousands) however it is worth doing. Most decorating companies would support you if you wanted to do this however, they may not pay

Site Manager

you for your day at college. Some would though, it depends on the company that you work for. In my experience, most companies would support you.

Once you have gained your HNC, you could go on to university and carry on studying part-time. This is a good idea. However, I would look to get a job as a junior site manager once I gained the HNC as the building company may then pay for your degree.

If you are serious about becoming a site manager then I would get the degree because this will make you more attractive to employers.

Route 3 — Working towards the role

If you are an older decorator or you don't fancy going back to college and studying again then this could be the route for you. You would need to work your way up through the ranks.

Become the site manager for the decorating company that you work for and get an NVQ (in site management) while you do the role. The assessor would come on-site and do this so there would be no need to attend college.

Once you are qualified get a job at a construction company and get a job as a site manager with them and then gain experience and go for promotion when it comes up within the company. If it is a growing company then there will be plenty of opportunity for you.

Site Manager

Route 4 — Applying directly

This is the most unlikely route but worth a try if you are a confident person who can pull off an interview.

Look for site manager jobs online and if you see a junior position then apply for it. You may have to flower up your CV a little but if you have gained some management experience as a foreman painter at your current company then that should be easy.

Depending on how many people apply for the job and how experienced and qualified the other candidates are then you could have a good chance.

Make sure that site management is for you.

Finally, I just want to chat about the role. The money is good, and it can be an interesting job. Depending on the size of the company that you work for you will be responsible for the smooth running of the work. You will deal with contractors from all the trades and co-ordinate the work.

This can be stressful as things don't always go to plan. You need to be organised and you need to be good with people. You need to handle an array of big personalities that construction attracts and get results.

If you are not good under pressure, then this is not the job for you. It is no good earning fifty grand a year if you have a nervous breakdown. Be honest with yourself. It is not an easy job, but it could be a rewarding one.

Check out the Chartered Institute of Building website for more information www.ciob.org

Chapter 16

Working for a paint manufacturer

Working for a paint manufacturer

One thing that I did not realise until I worked at college and dealing with paint manufacturers was how many jobs there are working for them. Many people in these jobs are decorators.

There are many large paint manufacturers out there, I have chosen just two, Crown and Dulux. The range of jobs for these guys goes from a driver to working behind the counter in a decorating centre. You could be a store manager. You could work as a product development decorator testing new products to see what they are like to use and how they stand up to wear and tear.

There are just too many jobs for me to discuss here, the best thing to do if you fancy working for Crown is to get a job in one of the decorating centres working behind the counter and work your way up. If you are keen, hard-working and willing to learn they will be prepared to support you with your journey to your perfect job.

Here is one job at Crown that I found:

Permanent Sales Assistant / Driver

£19,090 per annum

Crown paints are seeking to recruit a permanent sales assistant/driver to join the team based in Peterborough.

Working for a paint manufacturer

The role is a permanent, full time position working 40 hours a week (Monday – Friday and weekends on a rota basis). In return, we are offering you a salary of **£19,000 per annum** + bonus + excellent benefits package.

Are you passionate about providing an exceptional customer centric service, tailored to each individuals needs? Providing our customers with a trusted brand as well as the highest quality paint and sundry products is just the start. We are looking for individuals that not only have a passion for our brand, but for the socially responsible activities and initiatives that Crown Paints actively engage in.

What you can expect form this role

As a Sales Assistant/Driver you will work alongside the store team, collaboratively supporting our Store Manager, in delivering a sustainable and profitable sales growth for Crown Paints. A positive and motivated approach will be key contributing to the Peterborough store targets, driving innovative yet effective sales with our range of decorative paints and sundry items.

The Peterborough Crown decorating Centre (CDC) is a busy store and plays a pivotal role within our network, currently made up of 136 CDCs. Our customer base varies from passing one-off retail customers through to builders and trades people who hold accounts and maintain repeat business. A key part of your role will be to identify

Working for a paint manufacturer

potential new customers, establish positive relationships and open customer accounts regularly.

Although the pay is not amazing compared to what you can earn as a decorator some of the other benefits are good, see below from the same job advert.

- The opportunity to earn up to a 25% performance bonus each quarter
- 28 days basic annual leave each year (plus 8 bank holidays)
- A variety of discounts / vouchers on products that Crown supply
- A generous pension plan where the Company will match, and even double your contribution
- Multiple other benefits relating to your health and wellbeing

A 25% bonus could be an extra £4,750 per year, so that is not to be sniffed at. Plus, you get 36 days paid holiday which is also good. You also get a pension which I will discuss in the next chapter.

Here is another one from Dulux, this is for a store manager. I have chopped the advert up so you can see the best bits.

Dulux DECORATOR CENTRE

Working for a paint manufacturer

Job Reference: REQID3173_1591015118

Salary: £24000 - £25000 per annum

Salary per: Annum

Job Duration: Permanent

Job Start Date: ASAP

Job Type: Permanent

Job Location: Droylsden, Greater Manchester

Job Industry: Retail

Job Skill: Store Manager

Benefits include:

- No evening or Sunday shifts
- 25 days holiday
- Up to 50% off all products sold in store (including family and friends discount)
- A defined contribution pension scheme (where we pay in **double** the amount you do!)

As you can see the pay is much better, as you would expect for a store manager and the benefits are remarkably similar to Crown.

I know a few decorators who have gone to work for a paint manufacturer, and they enjoy the security and benefits of the job.

Maybe one to think about on that cold day in winter when working outside up a ladder.

Chapter 17

Retirement

Retirement

Why has he written a chapter on retirement? Is this what you are thinking? Well, I must admit I was not too sure about writing it myself. You see in my head I am still about 28 but really, I am at an age where I can retire.

When you are 16 and you start to work, the last thing on your mind is retirement. I mean, 30-year-olds look old to you, retirement is like a million years away, let's focus on more pressing matters like going on holiday to Amsterdam.

Let me tell you this, and I know you have been told a thousand times. In the blink of an eye, you will be 65.

When I used to teach apprentices at college, I would have the group for 3 years. One thing that I used to do on the first day was to explain what we would learn and then I used to wait until they were all quiet and click my fingers.

"In the blink of an eye these three years will be over," I would say.

Then after three years on the last day, I would click my fingers again and say, "Was I right? Did it go quick?"

I think they sort of got it. Most agreed that three years had gone quickly and that I was an amazing teacher. Oh, not the last bit. I added that bit myself.

The point is that time goes by quickly and before you know it climbing ladders is getting hard and your motivation

Retirement

starts to wane. You start thinking about a pipe and slippers.

Typically for me, I am not a great fan of working hard until you are 65 and then stopping altogether and watching the telly. I think it is a daft plan and I can't believe that everyone buys into it.

What I am about to talk about is not all my own thoughts. I have been influenced by an author called Tim Ferriss. He wrote a book called the "4-hour Workweek" and he changes the way you think about retirement. Check it out, I am not on commission, I am just a fan.

I was chatting to the guy that works in the office at the joinery company that our training academy shares a building with. He is called Gary.

I was returning to work after the Christmas holidays. I came into the academy to set up for a course at the weekend and Gary was there making himself a brew. We did the whole "Happy New Year" thing and then discussed how good it was to be back and how we were sick of eating, drinking and sleeping.

I commented that we need to get used to it because that is probably what we will be doing when we retire. He then made a comment that stuck with me. "Retirement is rubbish," he said.

It turns out that he retired when he was 45 and spent 5 or 6 years going on walks, reading and generally being a person of leisure. He found that it was not for him and he came back to work, by choice of course, and he was now happy in his work socialising with people and making a difference.

Now you may be different, but we don't really know until we get there. Imagine making loads of sacrifices in your life and telling yourself that it will be all worthwhile once you retire only to discover when you get there that not only are you nearly dead but retirement is rubbish as well.

Having said this, I would still get a pension plan together because you want to do it so that you can retire if you want. I would also have some mini-retirements along the way where you have some time out, maybe 3 months to do what you want to do. White water rafting, mountain climbing or just reading without the distraction of work.

Many things that you want to do are so much better done when you are young, so why wait?

The best thing to do in my opinion (and this is from someone who worked at a college all of his life, so hey, what do I know?) is to have your own business that pays enough to let you have time out when you want. Some subcontractors on site took 3 months off in the summer to go on a long holiday. They made enough money in the remaining 9 months to pay the bills.

Even though you have your own business you can still plan for that time when you want out of the system. People talk about retirement like it's something that you need permission to do but you don't.

Once you have an income that covers your living expenses without you working then you are done with work if you want to be. From then on you are doing things that you **want** to do and not what you **have** to do. Believe me that makes a big difference to your life.

Some people get to this stage at 20 and some never get there. The rest of us are somewhere in-between. All I am trying to say in a book about work is take some time out to think about the end of work, too. In some ways, it is just as important.

Chapter 18

Some final thoughts

Some final thoughts

Well, here we are at the end of the book. That means that you are still with me, which is always good to know. I never like to end the book talking about day-to-day things like work and jobs. I like to take the opportunity to discuss a couple of things that I think about from time to time.

First, it is important to think about what you are doing with your decorating career. In some ways, I am in a good position because I can look back on my life of 40 years in the trade and I have some perspective. This is something that you do not have when you are 20.

Throughout your life, you change as a person. You don't see it happening yourself because it happens too slow, but it does happen. Some things stay the same, your basic personality for example. But a lot of what is important to you when you are 8 is not important at all when you are 18. Things that keep you awake at night when you are 30 are irrelevant when you are 60. You get the idea, you already know this.

I will never forget a part-time teacher that I used to work with. He was called Norman. He had been teaching painting and decorating at Lancaster College, and he had taken early retirement at 55 and come to Preston to do some part-time teaching to give him something to do.

He taught graining and marbling on our decorative techniques course that was all the range in the early nineties. Lawrence Llewelyn-Bowen and all that.

Some final thoughts

He was a brilliant artist, very creative. A great guy actually who taught me a lot. He had been treated badly by the management at his previous college, probably because he was hard to manage. I think artists are.

One day, I was talking about all the things that I had to do because I was in charge of the decorating department, and he said: "You know, Peter, nothing really matters, tomorrow comes around just the same."

Oh wow, my 28-year-old self was so angry at this statement. Of course, it matters! It is my job, it is my career, it pays the mortgage, it feeds my family! How can he say nothing matters! Of course, it does.

I was mad about this for about 10 years. I never fell out with him though because he was a great guy to work with, but I just could not understand how he could think like that.

Guess what? Now I am 55 myself I understand what he meant. How scary is that? I know what "nothing really matters" means. He could never have explained it to my 28-year-old self, I just did not have the perspective on life.

Anyway, my main point is that you change, so you need to keep looking at what you do. If at 16 you decided to be a decorator and now you are 30 and you need more money, or you fancy a challenge then you can change and do this. This easiest way to do this is from within what you already know. This is one of the reasons that I have written this book: so that you can see what options you have.

Some final thoughts

Second, I want to talk about productivity. It's my pet subject but I think that it is important. Everyone I speak to, and this is not just decorators, want more money for doing less work. They talk about 4-day weeks but for the same money as they are currently on or a 5-day week but with a pay rise.

There is never any mention of an increase in productivity. While I was writing this book, I did extensive research on the construction industry and I discovered a few startling facts.

One I have already shared and that is 12% of new work is being done in the North West. This is my neck of the woods, so I suppose I am lucky to live in a powerhouse of the economy.

Another astonishing fact is that, in 2019, the construction industry is worth £110 billion, that's £110,000,000,000, a hundred and ten thousand million. I know, I can't get my head around it either. You could buy a few Big Macs for that, I can tell you.

It is 7% of the entire UK economy.

When you look at productivity rates across industries, they use the measure of output per hour in pounds. For example, the average across the whole economy is £33.50 per hour.

That means that in general people in the UK turn out £33.50 worth of stuff an hour. If we got our act together

Some final thoughts

and turned out 10% more stuff, then that would be an additional £3.35 per hour and the new number would be £36.85.

That does not seem a lot but a 10% increase in productivity is a big leap. That is because we think about our own work. We may do some decorating and charge say £600 for a week's work. If we get 10% more productive then that's an extra £60. Not massive but there. I think this means that we do not take it too seriously.

That is still £3,120 a year, every year too, so over 40 years it is £124,000 or the price of a small house. Makes you think.

But let's take a bigger example, Ford UK. In 2019, they sold 236,137 cars. At an average of £20,000 per car then that's £5,000,000,000. Five thousand million pounds.

If I went to the head of Ford and said that I had an idea that would make Ford UK 10% more productive and if it worked, I wanted a bonus of 10% of the increase in turnover. Just a one-off bonus, not every year. After the first year, Ford gets to keep all the extra money.

Are you still with me?

To cut a long story short my bonus would be £50 million.

Let's now look at some other industries in the UK to see how productive they are compared to the average of £33.50 per hour.

Some final thoughts

Farming is £47.40 per hour. Wow, that's a lot more than the average. Well done, farmers. They use big machines and farm massive fields, so that helps.

Manufacturing is £37.50 per hour, people like Ford cars come under this category. That's better than average but not massively.

Finance is £67.00 per hour, these guys turn out a lot of value per hour, that is probably why they earn the big bucks.

Construction is a pathetic £26.10 per hour. That's way below even the average.

Now let's say I come up with an idea to increase the productivity of construction by 10%. This would still leave construction a long way off the average of £33.50 but would place them at £28.71 per hour. For this, I want a one-off bonus of 10% of the increase in productivity.

My bonus would be around £1 billion.

Can you see why it bugs me how rubbish we are as an industry?

Why do we not bother too much? Well, if you look at average earnings across industries you find this:

The average is £512 per week

Finance is the highest at £650 per week (average don't forget)

Some final thoughts

Construction is £600 per week on average.

We do alright out of not being very productive. So maybe we don't bother too much. I think there is another reason too.

If a decorating company got 10% more productive who do you think would have to change the most, probably the decorators themselves, they would have to work more efficiently and maybe a bit harder.

Who would benefit the most, though? The owner probably. Would they share this bounty with the decorators? From what I have seen the answer is no.

So, to earn more money for working less we need to be more productive but to do this and benefit we need to own the decorating company. I think, too, that if we do own the company, we need to share the increase with all involved so that everyone feels the benefit and then has more of an incentive to change. This creates an upward cycle where everyone wins.

Maybe a wild fantasy that everyone shares in the rewards of all our efforts, but I will end the book on that thought. Maybe one day.

Other books by the author

Fast and Flawless

A guide to airless spraying

This is a chatty guide to airless spraying for decorators, decorating students and anyone interested in spraying with an airless system.

The book covers all aspects of the airless sprayer including the components of the system, the different systems that are out there to buy and setting up the system.

The book covers topics such as types of sprayers, essential equipment, using the equipment, masking, PPE and masks, a bit about paint, what to do when it all goes wrong, spraying in the real world and common paint defects.

Other books by the same author

Other books by the same author

Fast and Flawless Pricing

A guide to pricing and business for decorators

Are you a decorator that struggles with pricing?

Have you just set up in business and are looking for some pointers?

Are you an established business looking for some inspiration on how to move forward?

This chatty guide on pricing and business will gently guide you through the process of pricing a decorating job. It looks at the pitfalls of getting your pricing wrong and the advantages of having a good pricing system.

The book has been written by someone who has both been a decorator and taught decorating in a local college for most of his life.

Other books by the same author

Fast and Flawless Systems

A decorator's guide to planning and carrying out a successful job

This book looks at systems for decorators.

This book covers all types of systems from which paint to use on what surface to what order you should spray a room. The book also covers aspects of decorating that you may or may not be aware of such as painting uPVC, training, funding and marketing.

If you have read the other two books already then this is one is a must-read. If you haven't, then this book is a great place to start.

Other books by the same author

Tales from the building site

Lessons learnt when working on a big site

The author has spent many years working in the building trade as a decorator. During all those years he has seen things that have made him laugh and things that have made him tear his hair out.

There have also been many occasions that have made him proud to be part of it all. Here is a book for all you people in the trade and also for everyone else who wonders what goes on behind those big high hoardings that clearly state the public are not allowed in.

It is a warts and all look behind the curtain from the perspective of a decorator. Be prepared to be shocked, to laugh and to shake your head in disbelief.

Other books by the same author

Boat Life

The trials and tribulations of living aboard

Nothing to do with construction or decorating. I love boats, I have one and I have lived aboard myself, so this is an insight into the lifestyle.

This is a book for Boaters, written by a Boater. Pete Wilkinson has spent his whole life around boats and has owned a couple too.

The book looks at all aspects of boating including, what is the best boat to buy, where to look when buying a boat and do you build one or do you buy one?

The following questions are answered: Which is the best type of boat — wood, fibreglass or steel? Do you borrow money or save to get your boat? Do you move around or stay put? What is the essential kit needed? How do you keep her shipshape?

The book also looks at living aboard and gives an insight into the liveaboard life. The book also puts boating into the context of modern life and discusses the advantages of living onboard.

Finally, if you have wondered what goes on behind the curtain of a Boater's life then this book will show you.

Check out the website

If you are interested in being kept up to date with future books, or you just fancy the odd freebie, then subscribe on my website.

www.fastandflawless.co.uk

About the author

Pete Wilkinson has been a decorator all of his life. In his younger years, he worked for a medium-sized decorating company doing a wide range of work.

Then at the age of 27, he got a job teaching painting and decorating at a local college. These days he runs his own training company called PaintTech Training Academy.

When he is not working, he likes to spend time relaxing on his boat with his wife Tracey.

Printed in Great Britain
by Amazon